Wh

Want In A MAN

How To Become The Confident Man That Women Respect, Desire Sexually, And Want To OBEY...In Every Way

By Bruce Bryans

Legal Disclaimer

Although the information in this book may be very useful, it is sold with the understanding that neither the author nor the publisher is engaged in presenting specific psychological, emotional, or sexual advice. Nor is anything in this book intended to be a diagnosis, prescription, recommendation, or cure for any specific kind of psychological, emotional, or sexual problem. Each person has unique needs and this book cannot take these individual differences into account.

ISBN-13: 978-1482699777

ISBN-10: 148269977X

Introduction

You know what feels really good?

I'll tell you...

Being in an insanely fun and fulfilling relationship with an incredibly beautiful, intelligent, noble, loyal, and affectionate woman that literally treats you like her king! Her only desire is that she wants to be happy with you.

It doesn't matter if you're broke, sick, or even going bald; she's REALLY incandescently happy (her words, not mine) just being in your presence for no apparent reason whatsoever. She finds fulfilment while making you happy and she not only wants to see you succeed in life, but she sincerely wants to help you succeed as well.

You know what else feels really good?

It feels great to wake up every day with a ridiculous amount of self-confidence and ecstasy simply because you know without a shadow of a doubt that you're with a woman that deeply admires, loves, and respects you as a man and as her lover. It feels amazing to be with a woman who honestly feels that no other man out there can compare, in any way, to the one she's with.

In other words, she sees you as the perfect man for her, above all others, and better than all the rest. I should know, because this is exactly what my life presently looks like. I've found a woman that is truly right for me, and she's the only woman I want to be with.

And believe me, after you've experienced something like this for yourself, you'll understand why this book had to be written. I really want to share with you the secrets to becoming the kind of man that can attract and keep a high-quality woman in your life and have her treat you like royalty.

Trust me on this one; if you've never had a gorgeous and highly affectionate woman treat you like a king, you're definitely MISSING OUT.

But don't worry, with everything that I'm going to teach you in this book you'll also be able to become the kind of man that a really phenomenal woman will WANT to treat like a king. You too will know what it feels like to be the perfect man for that special woman in your life or even for the one that you want in your life.

Don't get me wrong here. Becoming a better man has nothing to do with being flawless or superior to other people in a prideful sense.

No.

Becoming a better man is all about transforming yourself into the kind of man that is perfectly right for the high-quality woman that you want or the wonderful woman that you're already with.

It's about tapping into your deep masculine energies and reaching your highest potentials as a man that can confidently lead and love an amazing woman in an amazing relationship. It's about reaching deep into a woman's mind to fully understand her deepest emotional needs and desires so that you can be the only man that can truly fulfill her physically, intellectually, and spiritually. It's a journey and a never-ending process because as a man, there's always room for growth and improvement.

Becoming a better man for the woman you want to attract or the woman you already love is all about masculine maturity and true commitment. It's truly a transformation into becoming the kind of man that a woman cannot deny. And the more you commit to this transformation, no matter how difficult or daunting the task, you will reap immense rewards in many areas of your life.

Honestly, no one man can or ever will be THE quintessential perfect man for every woman out there. It's just not possible. But if your focus is on becoming the perfect guy for the right woman, I must commend you for taking this journey. As men, we're quite infamous for refusing to ask for directions or advice even when we don't have a clue as to where we're going or what we're doing. We'd rather not suffer the shame of having to get help from someone else because we think we need to have all the answers.

Well, you don't have all the answers in life, and neither do I. However, I do have the answers that can help you with women and dating. In fact, I probably have answers to questions you didn't even realize you should be asking!

Seriously, I do.

And that's only because I've spent a great deal of

time and effort putting together what I believe is the ideal blueprint that any man can immediately use to transform himself into the kind of man that a good woman finds irresistible and irreplaceable. I really wanted to design a simple yet effective blueprint that any guy could follow if he wanted to truly understand what goes on in the mind of an amazing woman in order to figure out what she's really looking for in her "perfect guy."

But most importantly, I wrote this as a guide for my brothers, and also the male friends that I have so that they could have a chance to experience what I experience daily, which is the respect and love of a breathtaking, phenomenal woman.

I wasn't always the "relationship" type of guy. Sure, I've dated girls and grew up learning how to attract women, but they were never the kinds of women that I'd want to settle down with. And honestly, for years all I really wanted was to find a quality woman that I would want to settle down with to build a meaningful relationship and perhaps a marriage someday.

But you see; my problems back then were twofold.

First of all, for some strange reason, I could not seem to attract a relationship with the kind of woman that I really wanted to be with. I seemed to be lacking something intrinsic that made the really quality women just ignore me, and at first I couldn't figure out what it was.

Secondly, I had a lingering fear deep down inside that even if I'd managed to get a great woman in my life, I'd eventually lose her. I was a casual dater and drifter for so long that when it came to romance and relationships I didn't have a clue as to what it would take to build and keep a mind-blowing relationship with an amazing woman.

I had the fear of failure and rejection looming over me.

So, after countless relationship failures, rejections, and letdowns... I had had enough! I decided to go to work on myself.

And boy, did I go to work.

I became obsessed.

In the end, I've probably spent hundreds, if not thousands of hours trying to figure out how to become a better man. I wanted to become the kind of man that could attract and keep an amazing relationship with a phenomenal woman.

I worked to become the kind of man who was so sure of himself and his place in the world that he made himself a homing beacon for the right kind of woman. I persevered to become the kind of man that was a chivalrous and charismatic gentleman, but also a manly man of high character that exuded mature masculinity. All I wanted was to become the best version of my authentic self as possible.

And you know what...

I did.

It took me YEARS to learn and implement a lot of the things I'll share with you in this book. But I guarantee that it won't take you nearly as long as it took me. I had to learn everything from scratch and make sense of it for my particular situation. And I saw the task of becoming the perfectly RIGHT man for the RIGHT woman as a duty.

This is why it was imperative that I write this book for guys like you who either want to be the best possible man for their wives or girlfriends or who desperately want to become an irresistible catch to the right woman. But when I went about writing this book, I also wanted to stay away from teaching guys how to be manipulative because such techniques will not work on high-quality women. In fact, you'll end up scaring away the woman who is right for you if you don't learn how to build and maintain attraction in her NATURALLY as opposed to playing mind games with her.

Trust me; this book WILL change the way you think when it comes to making your ideal woman feel an intense desire for you. You'll become much more successful in maintaining the respect, admiration, love, and devotion of a GOOD woman. This is something that many men will sadly, never experience in their lifetime. Let's have a moment of silence for these poor guys.

...

And we're back.

Anyway, luckily you're not one of these unfortunate fellows. So dig in, and please use this book as a reference guide. As you read through it, have a clear intention of what it is that you're hoping to gain from it.

Try not to read it as if you were reading a novel, but instead refer to it as a guidebook whenever you need to refresh your memory on what it takes to become a better man for the woman that's right for you.

I sure do.

So have fun, and enjoy.

Table of Contents

CHAPTER 1:
The Feminine And Masculine Forces Of Attraction

The Attraction of Feminine Grace to Masculine Chivalry

What does Indiana Jones, James Bond, and Han Solo (don't pretend like you've never watched *Star Wars* before) all have in common? What they have in common is a masculine presence that cannot be denied by anyone. There's just something about their characters that women find undeniably attractive.

But what is it exactly?

Actually, it's nothing more than a simple combination of mature masculinity and romantic allure. They appear well-rounded, adaptable, and capable of handling just about any situation. They possess something that I refer to as *masculine chivalry*, and to a highly feminine woman it is VERY magnetic.

Although they are just characters from popular movies, don't be fooled. Even fictional characters can only become popular when we can truly relate to them. And in this case, the idea behind chivalrous male characters like these attracts both men and women. Men want to be them and women want to be with them, but why?

Here's the thing. An intelligent, attractive and confident woman that has her act together will find the masculinity of a <u>chivalrous man</u> highly attractive. In fact, it's much easier to build and maintain desire in a woman if you possess your own unique brand of masculine chivalry since it all happens *naturally*.

And we all know that you just can't fight nature.

So in order to maintain high levels of attraction in a relationship, a man must continuously work on increasing his masculine polarity.

Understanding Masculine Chivalry

Now, before I even attempt to explain to you what I believe is the key to attracting and keeping a great woman in your life, let me first say what masculine chivalry is NOT.

It is not bending over backwards so that a woman always gets what she wants from you.

It is not always putting her needs before yours so that she will fall in love you.

It is not being so patient and understanding that you tolerate utter disrespect and rude behavior from a woman.

It is not being a love-struck puppy dog that gives her flowers and candy in hopes that she'll love you forever.

It is not being a macho jerk that displays feats of strength in order to win a woman's heart.

It is not being her savior and knight in shining armor every time there's conflict or a challenge in her life.

It is not being a doormat that she uses to get her way.

It is not being a dominating man that rules her with an iron fist.

It is not being a "nice guy" with a heart of gold that only wants her love and affection.

And it is not being some swashbuckling character in a movie that goes through great lengths to rescue his woman from harm.

Okay, maybe it has a little to do with that last point, but let me explain.

Masculine Chivalry is essentially the perfect mix of manly virtues and courtly behavior as it relates to how you live your life and how you interact with women. It is the perfect combination of <u>masculine maturity</u> and <u>romantic seduction</u>.

The mature, masculine man is confident, poised, productive, assertive, and self-directed. The chivalrous man is courageous and empathic in that he knows when it is acceptable and necessary to go out of his way to improve the quality of life of those around him. This is the kind of man that sees the world as a place of abundance, and he goes about making it a better place for himself and others.

He doesn't need to be the center of attention, nor does he need the approval and praise of those he serves. And even though he takes on the task of providing amply for himself, his woman, and those he has accepted responsibility for, he does not see this as a chore, but as a duty that is worthy of him.

If I could sum up the feeling of masculine chivalry, it is this:

It is the sense of duty that a man feels deep within

himself to become his best so that he can give his best and feel satisfied that he is doing his best. He doesn't NEED to be approved, praised, or rewarded by anyone, but his satisfaction lies in overcoming fear and weakness while helping to rid the world of all that causes pain and suffering.

This kind of man is both a leader and a healer. He is devoted to the woman he chooses as he finds fulfillment in fulfilling her deepest desires to be loved, cherished, and appreciated both passionately and intimately.

Such is the well-rounded chivalrous man of exceptional character. As this is the kind of man who is not only a REAL man through and through, he's also interesting, fun, seductive, and VERY considerate of others. He is not a "nice guy" simply because he chooses NOT to suffer or sacrifice himself just so people will like him. He does the RIGHT thing as much as possible as opposed to the "nice" thing, even when it is difficult. But he is also not rude, crude, or vulgar in his demeanor, for no high-quality woman in her right mind desires such a man.

The man who embodies Masculine Chivalry is one who understands and VALUES commitment. First of all, he is committed to his principles. He lives his life by a strict code of honor. He is a man of high ideals and he values all that is good and noble in the world. This makes him noble, magnanimous, and gracious with others because he makes decisions based on unchanging virtues.

Secondly, he is committed to his purpose in life. He

lives to serve the world and to give the very best of himself in some productive pursuit. If he is a musician, he is devoted to bringing happiness to himself and others through beautiful sound. If he is a doctor, he is deeply passionate about his work and sees the healing of the sick as more than a job or a career. He sees it as a calling. In this way he is devoted not only to a vocation, but to his calling in life.

Thirdly, he is committed to his relationships. Such a man learns to develop empathy for others and he sees it as his duty to make the world a better place to live in for those that he loves. He abides by the golden rule that a man should treat others in the way he would like others to treat him. And with this in mind, he is proactive in treating his family, friends, and associates with respect, tolerance, and honor.

Such a man can be described as fearless, dutiful, valiant, civil, faithful, honest, and devoted. He is far from being cowardly, rude, and disloyal, as these are the qualities of the men that he fights daily to ensure that the world is made a better place for not only the noble, but for the weak, the helpless, and the delicate things in life.

The most phenomenal women in this world are HIGHLY attracted to such men. They are desperately waiting for more men to step up and transform themselves into the kind of men that they can give themselves to.

Yes, you heard me right. High-quality women are DESPERATELY waiting for men who embody masculine chivalry. Even if you're already in a relationship with an amazing woman, you can continually develop yourself into a better man and make her see you as an irreplaceable lover and leader. She'll find herself even more attracted to you as you take the path of masculine chivalry. And if she's truly a phenomenal woman you'll find yourself being treated like a king more and more every day.

And what guy in his right mind doesn't want that?

The Graceful and Feminine Specimen

I'm attracted to women who embrace their full femininity. I just can't help it. In fact, the woman I'm with right now (and in the future) exemplifies what I'm referring to.

I love the graceful, warm, and mysterious nature of a woman who can walk into a room and command attention without saying a word. I've been in situations where I just *knew* that a highly feminine, graceful woman was walking behind me, without even seeing her at first. I know it sounds kind of strange, but here's the thing. When you know what you're looking for it tends to jump out at you from all angles. And that's how I respond to highly feminine, passionate women.

They stand out from the crowd. Only until I was able to develop the kind of qualities that these kinds of women admire was I able to attract the kind of romantic relationship that gave me a sense of fun, freedom, and fulfillment.

Imagine being with a beautiful, intelligent, affectionate, and highly capable woman that you're highly compatible with and who treats you like a king. This is what I experience on a daily basis, and I love it.

But why am I mentioning this?

Well, because the kind of woman that usually has her act together, in that she loves herself, loves people, is honest, loyal, charming, seductive, intelligent, resourceful, and very attractive, is usually the virtuous, high-quality type that most men would give anything to be with and keep around in their lives. And get this...these kinds of women are undeniably attracted to a man who embraces his masculinity through a noble and chivalrous character.

Now, don't get confused here. Just because a woman embraces her femininity in a graceful manner doesn't mean that she is strictly a girly girl. In fact, she can be quite versatile. To be honest with you, a woman can be a sports chick, yoga chick, attorney, or entrepreneur and still possess feminine gracefulness. It's all about the way she carries herself. It's the things that she says and doesn't say to you and also how she behaves in social settings.

Her gracefulness shows in the way she treats the men in her life, all the way from her father to you. And only the most phenomenal women will treat men, especially the masculine and chivalrous ones, with respect and admiration for all that is good in them.

Feminine grace surpasses just her manners. In fact, her gracefulness stems from her own acceptance of who she is and what she wants out of life. She's comfortable with being a woman and embraces it fully. She can exude a kind of charm that most men, especially the masculine chivalrous type, find irresistible. She's happy being a woman, and she is happy to be with a man who gives her full reign to do so.

Attracting and keeping a woman like this will all depend on one thing. There's one thing that you possess as a man in which she's interested in more than anything else that you have to offer her.

And that one thing is essentially...your *character*.

What Women Really Want From Men

The age-old question that has been asked by men all over the world is this:

What is it that women want from us?

To be honest with you, the answers are endless. Because there are billions of women in the world they all may want different things, a lot of different things in fact. However, when it all boils down to it, a man is simply a man and a woman is simply a woman. Being the human creatures that we are, there are certain things that both men and women want that, for the most part, are non-negotiable.

These are the built-in needs that arise from both our primal desires and our human nature. It's important to base the question of what women want on a woman's primal desires and needs simply because the answer will always be the same, for EVERY woman. Basing our query on human nature and instinct will bring about a bit more consistency in figuring out exactly what it is

9

that a quality woman wants from and in a man.

So to simplify things a bit, the question that men should ask is this:

What things do women want from men that can be considered non-negotiable, universal, and primal?

Now that we have the RIGHT question, let me give you the RIGHT answer:

The main thing that a woman wants from a man is the experience of feeling like a woman. She wants to lose herself in her femininity, and the only way she can feel this feminine_experience is when a man acts like...a man.

There you have it. Hopefully, I just saved you from years and years of confusion and worry.

And if I did...you're welcome.

But seriously, women are feminine creatures by nature and instinctively desire to be treated as such, no matter what society may say. It's the natural order of things, and so the more feminine a woman feels around a man, the more comfortable, secure, and desirable she will feel. It is this experience of *feeling* like a creature of feminine beauty that women of today are yearning for from men.

Heard that?

The woman of your dreams is *yearning* for the kind of man that can make her *feel* like a woman. And she has no choice but to respond to the man that can trigger this *feeling* within her.

Ah, nature is a beautiful thing isn't it?

This means that by developing the kind of masculine qualities of character that a woman is HARD-WIRED to RESPOND to, you'll NATURALLY make yourself absolutely irresistible and irreplaceable to her.

The Masculine Character and Women

The more masculine a man is the more feminine he will make the women around him feel. And the term *masculine* in this case refers to a man's character and his behavior. The best way for a man to develop a more masculine disposition is to <u>consciously</u> go about building his character and improving his personality.

In other words, as a man, it's important for you to take control of your life, take responsibility for your thoughts and actions, and learn to properly manage your emotions. This is as straightforward as it gets.

If you want to really impress a woman, or rather, the ideal kind of high-quality woman that you want to attract, the first thing you must do is focus on *building your character* and making yourself much more masculine in a natural sense.

This is the single most important thing you can do in this life. Nothing is more attractive to a quality woman than a man who places a high value on things like honesty and integrity, and other qualities of a sterling character.

Women love strong masculine men. While this doesn't have much to do with physical strength per se

11

(although that does make a difference), it does include strength of character and resilience.

A woman wants to know that she can be sure of her experience with you. She wants to know that she can depend on you while times are good. For example, she wants to be sure of your ability to handle temptation if you're faced with the opportunity to do something underhanded in order to gain something you want. She wants to be sure of your *personal integrity* in that you won't do something that doesn't align with your beliefs just to make a profit or enjoy a moment of fleeting pleasure.

This is VERY important to her.

On the other hand, a woman wants to know that she can rely on you to handle conflict when times are bad. In other words, she wants to be assured that she's with a MAN through and through. She doesn't want to feel as if you might only be reliable when things are going well and then fall apart at the seams when conflict arises. You'll end up looking like an incompetent little boy, and trust me on this one, that isn't fun for any man.

A woman wants to know that you can make her *feel* desirable, secure, feminine, and beautiful. She wants to know that you're the kind of guy she can grow with, one who can help her grow and reach her full potential as a woman. And the more masculine you are in character, the easier it will be to *naturally* make her feel this way.

When it comes to romance, the masculine man is a chivalrous and irresistible lover to his woman. He knows how to fulfill her both physically and emotionally, and he makes it his duty to ensure that her deepest needs for physical and emotional intimacies are met consistently.

A worthy challenge for any man, is it not?

How to Build a Powerful Masculine Character

Character building for a man is perhaps the most important task he could ever undertake in his life. I know it was and still is, for me at least. As soon as I began to focus on changing certain aspects of my character, I began to see the results in my life change as well. And believe it or not, the kind of life you lead and the kind of woman you'll attract and keep will all depend on who you are as a man.

All of your results in life will be based on who you are at your core as a man. Your train of thought, your automatic reactions to situations, and how you deal with conflict and other people are all linked to your character. Women are much more attracted to a man's character and personality than by his looks, possessions, or achievements. High-quality, intelligent women who have experience in dealing with men tend to have an inherent ability to see a man for what he truly is on the inside.

Armed with this knowledge, it is of best interest for you to focus on the development of your character and personality first and foremost. This is just a starting point, but for the sake of helping you to get your feet wet, here are a few manly character-building tips:

1. Start a new challenging hobby, something that you can see yourself becoming really good at. This will build your own manly confidence and it will also help you to develop discipline as you hone your skill or increase your knowledge in a new area.

2. Develop a new skill or an old talent and use it as a means to further you in your career or build a business. This will help you to take conscious control of the self-development process by forcing you to hone your mental faculties to be creative in your work.

3. Travel with your woman often and plan unforgettable experiences with her. Take the initiative and make it your business to ensure that her life is filled with romantic fun and adventure. This will help you to develop your organizational and creative capacities where your woman is involved.

4. Set a challenging goal for yourself and commit to attaining it. This will help you to build character and will show your woman that you are goal-driven and ambitious.

5. Join a gym or sports team or pick up a martial art and develop your body. This is a sure way to both build your own manly confidence while impressing your woman with your new physique and skill. It will also help you to develop self-discipline as becoming competent in any kind of workout, sports, or martial arts will require great amounts of effort and persistence.

6. Read more books that will propel you forward in life. Try to get more reading done in the year. Any book that will aid in your personal development (like this one) will help you to build a stronger character by sharpening your mental faculties and your ability to solve problems.

7. Find some friends that will help you excel in life. Join a social club where men gather and find ways to add value to the gathering and to your community. This will help you to grow in character as you are forced to learn how to relate better with other men in order to get your needs met and the needs of others by working together.

8. Be creative in your love life and treat your woman as if she were the most important person on earth (isn't she?). Come up with fun and creative ways to show your affection on an on-going basis. This will help you to develop the virtues of love and gratitude, as the more you pour yourself into the relationship, the greater rewards you will reap.

9. Take charge of situations on your job or at home. Offer up suggestions to solve conflicts, be the first one to make a move, and take more initiative. Learn to become a masterful decision-maker. This will help you to develop the masterful quality of personal initiative. A trait that is common in ALL leaders in every walk of life.

10. Go above and beyond the call of duty in your love life and develop your manly resourcefulness in your relationship. Learn what really makes your woman tick and ensure that her needs are met even before she realizes she had one. This will help you to develop the habit of going the extra mile and over-delivering on your promises and commitments.

Those suggestions should be more than enough to

help get you started.

Even though they're all pretty useful suggestions, you've got to do the work. Start with something and commit to seeing it through. Take action now, and challenge yourself. It's the ONLY way to build the kind of character that you want and that the woman of your dreams NEEDS from you, as building character is important for any man who is looking to create more desire in his woman, and more happiness in his own life.

When a man goes about his life consciously building his character and making himself and the world around him a better place, he shows his woman that he is a man through and through, and that she can count on him in times of need.

The Key to Her Heart: Earning and Keeping Trust

A woman can only love and respect you as a man as far as she can trust being with you. It's as simple as that my friend. Believe me, it's impossible to truly love and appreciate your woman and get her to do the same if she cannot put her trust in you.

Above all else, she *needs* security from you.

This is why women have the habit of testing men, day in and day out. It's almost a subconscious habit that's built in to their psyche. They test men in order to be sure of what their experience with him will continue to be. And they will continue to test men throughout their lives to ensure that they can still rely on him in the bad times as well as the good.

You should keep in mind that these tests aren't really meant to cause you any unwanted stress or drama in your life, but they're really meant to keep you on your toes. They're meant to reveal to her the truth about who you say you are and who you're trying to be. To put it simply, a woman will test you to examine and assess the nature of your character.

At first, it may be easy for you to get by on your personality alone. You can be as charming and as dashing as you want, but in the long-run your true character will reveal itself. Every competent, high-quality woman is fully aware of this.

Her Experience with You

What a woman wants to be sure of more than anything is her experience with you. This goes beyond her physical senses in that she wants to feel secure with you in mind, body, and soul. She wants to know how you'll deal with her emotional nature and she wants to know if she can rely on you when the going gets tough.

What she really wants is a feeling of security, knowing that no matter what life throws her way you'll be there as a source of strength and encouragement. She wants to feel secure in your ability to weather the storms of life.

A woman is naturally hardwired to seek out power and security simply because it's a part of her survival. At times of course, you'll come across those women who take this to the extreme, but it's quite natural for a woman to want a certain level of security.

This is why an intelligent, high-quality woman will not only be highly attracted to a man with a strong character, but she'll become highly invested in a man who has ambition and drive. Without this certainty, a woman will not be attracted to you, or if she finds out that you're incapable of making her feel secure over the long-term, she cannot remain attracted to you.

This is simply her survival instinct at work within her. She can't control it.

Yeah I know; it's tough being a guy. But it's all about embracing the challenge my friend. That's exactly the kind of attitude that a woman will find highly attractive and desirable in a man. It is his strength of character and his ability to deal with conflict that will determine just how much she can trust you.

The safer a woman feels with you, the more she will open up to you. And she will open up to you in mind, body, and soul while being more than willing to follow your lead as long as she can place her complete confidence in you.

Be Decisive, Handle Conflict, and Stay Calm

Okay, so you've probably realized about now that a man's character is the most important factor in determining how much a good woman will love, trust, and respect him. It's the key component in getting a woman to have faith in your brand of love and leadership.

Don't get me wrong, an attractive personality does count for a lot, but it's more like the icing on the cake. In other words, personality is a great way to attract and entice a woman, but it's your character that will make her trust and respect your leadership, and make her desire everything that you have to offer. Assuming you want this one of a kind woman in your life for a long time to come, your character is the ONLY thing that will make her STAY for the long haul.

Now, here's my number one tip for developing the kind of character that a woman finds overwhelmingly desirable:

Become secure in your ability to make intelligent decisions in the face of conflict, and become a master at handling your emotions.

Here's the thing, it's impossible for a woman, or anyone for that matter, to put their trust in you in any situation if you cannot trust yourself. As a matter of fact, women have an innate ability to pick up when a man is being indecisive, and they can smell a lack of confidence on a man as if it were rotting flesh.

You don't want her to smell rotting flesh. Do you?

No, you don't.

The more control you exert over yourself, especially in times of conflict, the more attractive and desirable you will be to a woman. This applies the same whether you're in a serious relationship or single.

The best part about this is that she cannot control it. A woman has no control over her ability (or inability) to feel a sense of attraction or admiration for you if you become a master at managing your own emotions. She'll see you as a source of strength, and it will make it much easier for her to place her trust and security in you.

The Unforgivable Sin That Can Ruin Everything: Your Own Insecurities in Being with Her

Why is it that a woman, especially a good woman, cannot stand an indecisive man? Why is it that a man who displays a lack of confidence is a complete turn off to her? How is it that an anxious and timid man will literally make a woman cringe and run in the opposite direction? And why does a man who lacks ambition have zero chance with a great woman?

These are all valid questions my friend, so I'll tell you.

It's because all these things show that such a man is *insecure* with himself and his ability to make decisions, to commit to anything, and to lead her. And guess what? She's been biologically designed by her Creator to avoid these kinds of men. She MUST learn to avoid these kinds of men simply because if she and her offspring are to survive it's not in her best interest to date and mate with these imposters.

Insecurity in all of its various forms will cause a woman to become unsure about you. If she becomes unsure about your ability to lead, love, and take care of her emotionally and physically, she will eventually lose the respect and desire she has for you. It's not that she doesn't want to trust you; she has no choice in the way she *feels*. It's how she was designed by nature.

How Nature Designed Her

The confident guy gets the girl because she needs security.

The financially successful guy gets the girl because she needs security.

The physically fit and handsome guy gets the girl because she needs security in knowing that her offspring will be strong and healthy.

The decisive and determined guy gets the girl because she needs security in knowing that he can lead.

In other words, she's *designed* to seek out the kind of man she can place her *confidence* in. And the only way she's going to place her confidence in you and continue to do so will be based on your ability to deal with your inner conflicts and insecurities as a man. This is why it's so important for a high-quality woman to find a man who has a set of morals and principles that he follows diligently.

If a man has a set of ideals that he holds more important than anything else in his life, his decision-making will be based on something that is essentially unchangeable and that cannot be easily corrupted or distorted. The basis for his decision-making and therefore his actions are set in stone. A great woman will give her all to a man that has a concrete system of ethics that he follows religiously.

In short, the ideals and values you live your life by will help you to deal with your inner conflicts and insecurities because your decision-making won't be guided by how you *feel* at the moment.

This is very important here.

A woman knows on an unconscious level that she is an irrational creature. She knows that most of the time her emotions will get the best of her, and that she makes decisions based mainly on how she *feels* at that very moment. This is a beautiful thing because this is what makes her a feminine creature. But the mere fact that she instinctively knows that she was made this way, she will naturally seek out a mate who is strong and confident and who does not make decisions based on the push and pull of emotions alone.

In other words, a heterosexual woman of high-quality really doesn't want to be in a relationship with another woman. She wants a man, the kind of man that is led by unchanging ideals, values, principles, and ethics. She wants a man who follows a code, and who doesn't deviate from that code no matter the circumstance.

Finding such a man is important to her survival, and she instinctively knows this. This is why when you become insecure about something she may begin to lose faith in you. To put it simply, when you begin to waver and become self-doubting about your ability to fulfill her needs…her survival is now at stake.

Take Control of Your Emotions

We all have our insecurities in some form or another. You're a human being and that's fine. But here's the thing, it's not the insecurities that are the problem, it's how you deal with them as a man. Do you hide them deep within yourself and whenever pressure is applied they spring up and manifest themselves in some uncontrollable outburst? Maybe you try to play off your insecurities by playing tricks or lying to yourself? Or do you just let your insecurities get the best of you in any situation and you have no control over your own actions?

It's all about how you deal with them that matters.

If something is really bothering you and you want to get it handled, don't be ashamed to get help. A great starting point is to get books on the issue that you may be dealing with. A good book can do wonders for helping you to solve your inner conflicts, and there are thousands of self-help books that can give you some pretty rock solid advice.

Also, if there is someone you trust that can help you with an issue, then don't be afraid to ask them for help. If it seems to be a serious relationship or intimacy issue, I'd advise counselling or pastoral help as opposed to just anybody. Or better yet, be open and honest about it with the woman in your life.

A good woman is one that will support you even though you may have weaknesses and emotional insecurities. And her supporting you will be based on how you decide to deal with your inner conflicts.

Remember that becoming a better man isn't about becoming Mr. Perfect. No man is flawless in every area of his life, and a really good woman knows this. But believe me, an intelligent, quality woman can tell when you're hiding something or trying to keep a deep-rooted issue under wraps.

It's better to be honest about something that you're uncomfortable with than to just let something get out of control later on. If she sees that you're trying to help yourself, a good woman will want to help you as well. This is especially true if she realizes that even with your inner conflicts you're still exercising self-discipline by adhering to the principles that you live by.

This is the beauty of having a set of standards to follow because your insecurities and personal issues will never dictate your decision making. No matter what our inner conflicts are as men, and no matter what may be going on around us, as long as we allow our thoughts and actions to be based on sound principles for living successfully we'll always come out on top. Always remember...

A good woman loves a man who lives by virtue and not merely by his emotions alone.

This is what she wants in a man and this is the kind of leadership she will rely on in a relationship. It will provide her with the security she requires, and she will consistently place her faith in your ability to fulfill her needs.

CHAPTER 2:
How To Become The Man That She Needs

How to Be and Remain THE MAN When Relating with a Woman

First things first, I have some bad news for you.

Are you ready for it?

Well, the bad news is that your nice guy persona is actually ruining your chances of building and maintaining attraction with a woman. And if you're already in a relationship with a good woman it may be causing her to lose her respect, desire, and admiration for you.

I told you it was bad news.

But never fear because the good news is that you can change your nice guy persona, take charge of your life, and have the kind of fulfilling relationship that you both will enjoy immensely. Trust me, a good woman WANTS you to grow a pair...and hold onto them. Your wife or girlfriend does NOT want you to give your power over to her. In fact, this is the one thing that if you give it to her she will undoubtedly, without question, LOSE her respect and attraction for you on every level. I don't know how to explain it any better than this.

Sure, you might be saying to yourself that women like being with nice, sweet guys and that you may even know a few nice guys in what may seem like successful relationships. Let me educate you here buddy, and listen to me carefully... If you want to remain in a healthy, meaningful, and fulfilling relationship with a phenomenal woman who wants nothing more than to treat you like a king and to be treated like royalty as well, then you're going to have to learn how to go from Mr. Nice-guy to Johnny Bad-guy in a heartbeat <u>when it's necessary</u>.

Don't worry, becoming the "bad guy" doesn't mean you have to change who you are. In fact, being yourself is all about becoming more authentic with what you're really all about. It is essential in attracting and keeping a woman that is right for you.

Now, there are certain aspects of yourself that may need to be improved upon if you're going to transform into the BEST version of yourself. This is the very same version that is the perfect match for the woman that you really want or the woman that you're already crazy about. But I think it bears repeating: a high-quality woman wants nothing to do with a "nice guy". Don't worry; I'll be more than happy to explain to you why this is. Since in all honesty, I myself had to change my "nice guy" ways as well.

3 Reasons Why No Woman in Her <u>RIGHT</u> Mind Wants to Be With Mr. Nice-Guy

The title pretty much says it all. But I'll reiterate just in case you might have missed it.

No good woman in her RIGHT mind wants to be with a Mr. Nice-Guy.

I expect that if you are a nice guy, this may be pretty hard for you to swallow right now. Don't worry;

I'll give you a moment to take it all in.

Okay, moment's up.

Let's get back to reality.

I'm going to try to explain exactly why a quality woman is not going to want to end up with a Mr. Nice-Guy unless she is completely out of options, hopeless, and somewhat desperate. If this is the case then I guess it's safe to say that she may not be that much of a quality woman after all. But in any event, here are the reasons why nice guys are more often than not, rejected, dumped, and cheated on by the women who ARE in their right minds:

1. Nice Guys Have Difficulty Doing the RIGHT Thing

Yeah, you heard me right. Nice guys have a lot of difficulty doing what is right in a particular situation. Instead of doing what's right, nice guys tend to opt for the much easier route and decide to do what is nice. If you can't do the right thing then that means you make decisions based on trying to keep everyone else happy instead of ensuring that you'll be happy with yourself if you looked in the mirror.

A woman who has her act together won't tolerate this because this will make you a pushover to her and anyone else. She'll see you as the kind of guy that is easily led by others and who is incapable of taking the necessary actions to makes things right in any given circumstance.

If you are a nice guy that does the nice thing as opposed to the right thing, she'll simply see you as being unreliable. She'll realize that you won't be able to handle the conflicts of life and that you won't be able to act with personal integrity. If you lack personal integrity that means you lack self-respect. Believe me, no woman can truly admire or respect a man in the long-run if he cannot respect himself.

2. Being Mr. Nice Guy Makes You Seem Less Authentic

As a man, it's important to be as authentic as possible in the choices that you make. It's simply a part of being a mature man. But nice guys tend to have a problem with authenticity because they will say yes to just about any request that comes their way. Nice guys also have a difficult time sifting through the enormous amounts of demands upon their time and resources. Because of this a woman can never be too sure of what is authentic about him and what isn't.

In other words, nice guys allow too many unnecessary commitments into their lives. Their lives are simply filled with too much "fluff". They deal with other people's burdens, other people's demands, and other people's plans. Nice guys place themselves second to everything and everyone else, and that usually makes them a dumping ground for others.

You can be assured that no woman is going to want a man who's a dumping ground for someone else. If you can't be true to yourself, a woman will simply feel as if you won't be true to her. She won't be able to feel secure with you, and thus her ability to become intimate with you will be extremely limited, if at all possible.

3. Nice Guys Give Their Power Away to Women

If you're a nice guy, chances are you've been giving your power away to women and not even realized it. You've probably been allowing women (mother, sister, wife, girlfriend, etc.) to make the most important decisions of your life, and even the not-so important ones as well. You've probably developed a kind of relationship with women whereby you need to have them be happy with you in order for you to be happy with yourself. And believe me; you don't want to be in this kind of situation.

Why? Well, if a woman senses that you easily give your power away to her, she may realize that you may do it for another woman as well. She'll wonder what makes her so special anyway. What she wants is a man in control of himself, and at times, *her as well*. Giving your power away to a woman simply means that you give her the permission to approve of you and that you've given her the pleasure of ensuring that your needs are always met.

This is a no-no.

Once again, no woman in her right mind wants a man to give his power away to her. She will feel forced into the position of being the "man in charge" and she won't like it. In fact, she despises it. And even worse, she despises men who make her feel that way.

Why Nice Guys Never Win With Women

Remember how no woman in her right mind would want to be with Mr. Nice-Guy? Well, luckily for Mr. Nice-Guy we have lots of women out there who are not entirely in their right minds at all. This is actually great for our friend Mr. Nice-Guy because he can still put other people's needs before his and maintain a relationship with a woman. But what kind of woman will he attract or even *create* exactly?

Because of the way nice guys treat people, they tend to attract various kinds of women that may prey upon their gullible, naive, and overly kind-hearted ways. Even worse, they end up *creating* women like this as they become passive in their relationships. They may attract women with all sorts of issues, everything from emotionally needy women to gold-diggers. You'd be surprised at the kinds of women that nice guys NATURALLY attract without even realizing it.

There is an old cliché that suggests that there is someone out there for everybody. I believe it's kind of true since a nice guy and his manipulative ways can find some measure of what he thinks is happiness in a relationship with an equally manipulative woman that really wants to dominate or control the relationship. But no man in his right mind would want to be in a relationship with a damaged and manipulative woman.

Don't get me wrong here, I understand that no one is perfect and that everyone is going to have their own issues in a relationship, but that doesn't mean that you should go out looking for the worst of the bunch since you do have the choice to avoid it.

For example, a nice guy may attract an extremely possessive woman that will place high demands on his time and resources. Being the nice guy that he is, he'll learn to put up with her high demands in order to keep her happy thinking that he's doing the right thing when in fact he's simply doing the nice thing. All the while he's actually suffering inside, getting fed up and internally conflicted with trying to please this woman and trying to keep himself sane and happy.

This guy is essentially suffering because of his lack of personal boundaries. The more he overlooks her behavior and accepts it as something that he has to deal with, the more he will suffer internally and begin to dislike the woman and worse...himself. If he cannot respect himself, no woman can respect him. The nice guy may soon learn that without self-respect, he can never find true happiness in a relationship with his ideal woman.

In short, a high-quality woman loves and wants a man that has a high sense of *self-respect*. It's a necessity. A low-quality woman on the other hand, one who will waste your time and resources, is a woman that a self-respecting, high-status man simply cannot develop a meaningful relationship with. The two will be completely out of alignment with one another simply because a man with a high-level of self-respect and personal boundaries needs a woman who also shares the same qualities.

Make no mistake; a man who considers himself

high-quality needs to be with a woman who knows how to respect his personal boundaries. Anything less will be unfulfilling, unsatisfying, and completely unsustainable to him.

10 Things You Should Know About the Nice Guy

Before we can go about solving a problem let's make sure that there actually is one. So before I show you how to go about getting rid of your Mr. Nice-Guy persona, let's see exactly how much of these nice guy behaviors and beliefs you do actually struggle with.

Here are ten things you MUST know about the Nice Guy:

1. The nice guy believes that if he is good, giving, and caring, he will get happiness, love, and fulfillment from others in return. He plays a sort of game with himself thinking that he deserves to be treated a certain way because of his niceness.

2. The nice guy offers to do things for a woman he hardly knows when he wouldn't normally do it for just anybody else he knows. He has a strong desire to gain the approval of women. This can be any woman, especially ones that he finds appealing and worthy of his excess amounts of niceness.

3. The nice guy avoids conflict by withholding his opinions or may even become agreeable with a woman when he doesn't actually agree. This nice guy tends to think that in order to keep the peace and maintain the love and admiration from a woman, he must agree with her at all cost. He does this even if it costs him his self-respect.

4. The nice guy tries to fix and take care of all her problems. He is drawn to trying to help a woman out in any way that he possible can. This is one of the main reasons why a nice guy tends to attract a lot of damaged women. His desire to be her Mr. Fix-It makes him susceptible to fall into relationships with problematic women.

5. The nice guy has an overpowering need to seek approval from other people. It's the kind of approval seeking whereas he may feel guilty for saying "no" to someone or he may become uneasy with himself when he's rude, even if it's out of necessity.

6. The nice guy tries to hide his perceived flaws and mistakes from others. Because he wants everyone's approval and he wants to be seen in the best light possible, he's willing to go to extreme lengths to make himself look as flawless as humanly possible. He's manipulative to the third degree.

7. The nice guy is always looking for the right way to do things as opposed to just making an attempt at something. The nice guy is afraid of failing and of course, making a mistake in front of others. He doesn't want to step on anyone's toes. Because he doesn't want to rock the boat, he'd rather not do anything if he doesn't have all the answers. Sadly, his fear of failure and criticism culminates in pointless perfectionism and perpetual procrastination. He does nothing, and accomplishes less than nothing.

8. The nice guy tends to over-analyze everything rather than feel things out for himself. Sometimes the nice guy can be a bit of a perfectionist, and instead of just going with the flow and just letting things happen he'd rather have everything planned out and accounted for in his own perfect universe.

9. The nice guy has difficulty in making his needs a priority. Instead he'd rather pretend that what he wants isn't that important and that he's being a team player. Or he'll think that by putting his needs on the back burner he's being one hell of a guy and that everyone should always remember that he's such a great guy and that everyone should like him.

10. The nice guy is quite often emotionally dependent on his woman. He's so dependent on his woman for his own emotional well-being that he'll go through great lengths to ensure that his woman's needs are met before his and that he always gets her approval. Because in the end, he knows that as long as she's happy, he's happy.

Why You Must Kill the Nice Guy Inside

When life pushes you around do you push back or lie on your back and take it? Do you wait around thinking to yourself that people should treat you better and that things should always go your way, or do you get out of your comfort zone and expand your own person boundaries? Are you confident enough to go out and try, and at times fail, to get your needs met or do you sit by the wayside waiting for the scraps of life and love to be handed out to you? What have you done lately to expand your capacity for problem solving and handling conflict?

Depending on how honest and humble you are with yourself while answering those questions, it may be time for you to _KILL_ your Mr. Nice Guy. Have no fear; I'm here to help you through the process since I've learned how to murder my own Mr. Nice Guy repeatedly whenever he decides to show up. Yes, it will make you uncomfortable, but that's just the point. Don't worry; I'll walk you through it.

How to Stop Being a Mr. Nice Guy

First thing you should do is to learn the traits of a nice guy and become fully aware of when you or some other guy is acting like one. Learn to become conscious of your behavior, as this is the first step to changing the unproductive way you respond to people, especially women.

The second step is to become fully honest with yourself and analyze yourself to see which of the nice guy qualities apply to you the most. It's unlikely that you're a complete pushover when it comes to your relationships, as most nice guys tend to be at different points on the nice guy scale. Figure out which behaviors are almost instinctive to you, and catch yourself in the act.

As you interact with people, especially women, pay attention to yourself and what you say and do to avoid conflict and confrontation. Catch yourself in the act of being inauthentic with people in order to avoid hurting their feelings. See yourself in the act of doing the nice thing instead of the right thing and begin to consciously choose the more difficult route.

Instead of taking the nice way out, challenge yourself consciously. Make the effort to get out there and get your needs met. This isn't an invitation to be a complete jerk mind you, but it is a call to man up! It's okay to start small.

For example, instead of being a *yes man* by mindlessly agreeing with someone, try saying something like, "You know, I respectfully disagree. In my humble opinion I think she's a rather excellent up-and-coming musician. She's a new artist for sure, but I think she has so much more potential."

Of course, you don't need to use my brand of dialogue to make your point, but it shows that you can disagree with someone without being disrespectful. You can be your own man and have your own opinion and still be...*nice*.

And finally, you must be prepared to follow through with your desire to assert yourself CONSISTENTLY. This is how you form a new habit. You must continue to assess your behaviors in various social situations and consciously choose the more bold and assertive route as opposed to your normal passive behavior.

Remember to use common sense in this regard as well. You're not trying to be disagreeable for disagreeing sake. If you disagree you should have a valid point to make, or if you're asserting yourself then you should be trying to get your needs met without encroaching upon the rights and well-being of others.

Don't be ashamed or embarrassed to ask for what you want or to have a firm opinion about something. That's either foolish pride or false humility stopping you. And you'll find that nice guys have far too much of both.

A Simple Technique For Quitting Your Nice Guy Habits

The best piece of advice I can give you for consistently keeping your Mr. Nice Guy at bay is this...

Turn the art of disappointing people and putting your needs first into a practice. In other words, make it a discipline, a ritual, a way of life.

When you find that disappointing someone is a <u>necessity</u> because it's not a win-win situation for either of you, look at the opportunity as a chance to build your self-esteem and assert yourself. If you think of it as a practice or a discipline, you'll be comfortable when you fail from time to time. But on the other hand you'll also realize that with each conscious attempt you're actually getting much stronger as a man. Always keep in mind that the practice of disappointing people in order to be authentic with yourself and others will strengthen your personal boundaries.

And even though the thought of people not liking you may tempt you to take the nice way out, just remember that in most cases when you do stand up for yourself and act assertively in your relationships, people will respect you and you WILL gain confidence in the long run.

By the way, best-selling author, Dr. Robert Glover,

wrote a book called, *No More Mr. Nice Guy*. It's a life changing, paradigm-shifting, kick-in-the-groin kind of book that will challenge you and help you to overcome your "nice guy" issues. I believe ALL men should read and apply it to their lives. In fact, if you feel that you experience seemingly overwhelming conflicts in life due to your "nice guy" tendencies, I HIGHLY recommend that you check it out.

Stop Living for a Woman's Approval

If you're presently living for a woman's approval you're probably not one of the happiest guys around. Every day that goes by and you seek a woman's approval, a little bit of your inner manliness dies. You end up with a deep-rooted feeling of powerlessness and suffering, and you're too conflicted to do anything about it. Or perhaps, you're just unaware of what's really going on inside of you.

As a man you were meant to be self-reliant, independent, and highly capable at leading yourself and your family in the best way you possibly can. But when you go about your life seeking the approval of women you actually end up losing these qualities. You actually end up giving up your *rights* as a man, and therefore you'll find your life heading in a direction you never intended it to.

Simply put, the more you seek approval from women the more you're going to malfunction as a man. This sort of malfunctioning can lead to all sorts of relationship and even work-related problems.

How to Stop Seeking a Woman's Approval by Becoming Comfortable with "NO"

The most valuable thing you can do for yourself right now as a mature man who wants to become a better man for the woman you want is this:

Become comfortable telling people NO, and hearing NO from others.

Honestly, if you followed just this one piece of advice, you my friend are on your way to a much happier and successful life not only with women but in every other relationship. *No* is a wonderful word. It's a good thing. And yes, I know we live in a world that promotes saying *yes* to life and having a positive mental attitude, but saying *no* to others, to yourself, and hearing *no* and becoming comfortable with it will make you feel much more powerful and in control of your life.

Learning to be comfortable with *no* will help you to get over the idea of needing the approval from other people. It's probably the fastest way to become a more mature, confident, and self-assured man. I assume this is your goal, is it not?

Becoming a *no* man doesn't mean you're becoming selfish and self-centered. In fact, learning to become comfortable with saying *no* and hearing the word *no* will make you much more generous, forgiving, patient, and understanding of others. You'll learn how to focus on win-win solutions in your relationships and your ability to influence others will increase exponentially.

Make no mistake, the only way you can really help others is if you're free from their approval. It's impossible to authentically help someone if you need them to like you. You can't have both. So learn to become ridiculously comfortable with people NOT liking you. One of the best ways to do this is to become a *no* man yourself.

Why Telling Her "NO" Makes Her Happy

A high quality woman is much more attracted to a man who knows what he wants and is determined to get it. She admires and respects a man who follows his inner convictions irrespective of what others may think. She'll gladly follow a man who can tell her *no* when she needs to hear it.

A woman, knowing that she can sometimes be an emotional and irrational creature, will unconsciously *want* and *desire* a man who can put her in her place when the time comes. It's important to her survival and to that of her offspring because it means that you show courage and integrity in sticking to your inner convictions.

She'll know that you respect yourself first and foremost and that you're more than willing to assert yourself and stand your ground if you feel as if your personal boundaries are being imposed upon. If you can stand up for yourself, she'll know that you can stand up for her as well.

The more self-respect she sees that you have for the fulfillment of your own needs, she'll also realize that you'll be more than capable at fulfilling her own. But in order for her to see this quality you must REFUSE to be a doormat for other people, including her, by asserting yourself. Timidity will get you nowhere if you want to become the kind of guy that can both attract and keep a high quality woman in your life. You need to have guts and iron nuts to say *NO*.

Knowing When to Say "No" to NO and "Yes" to YES

When you come across a woman that you're interested in and you're getting to know her a bit more in a dating relationship, think of saying *no* as a way to qualify her for greater access to more of you.

Don't just give her everything she asks for at the beginning. The word *no* should be used to communicate your personal boundaries and that you only let people have access to more of you (your intellect, your time, your social circle, your emotions, etc.) when you find them agreeable to your values and standards.

As you build a meaningful relationship with a woman it's important to know WHEN to say *no* and when to say *yes*. It's all about balance, and understanding the importance of being clear about what you will or will not tolerate from others. In order to become intimate with another person you must be willing to sacrifice and compromise.

But always remember that such things are best done in a relationship that is based on mutual respect and commitment between two people. In other words, saying *yes* should always lead to win-win outcomes.

Become a Mature Man by Embracing Opposition

Learning to embrace conflict, challenge, and obstacles in the form of the word *no* will make you stronger. Opposition will bring out the fight in you and make you more resilient. Being turned away, rejected, and disliked by others will assist in strengthening a mature and masculine character in you so long as you keep striving to get your needs fulfilled.

Accepting that there are probably only select groups of people who will want you to succeed and be happy and help you along the way will help you to free your mind from having to be liked by others. If you're a real people pleaser and all-around nice guy that allows people to have their way with you, learning to embrace *no* will help you to become a more assertive man that a woman will love.

You should let the word *no* become a source of motivation for you in life. Use oppositions in the form of *no* as a way to propel you towards your goals in life. It will help you to develop a "damn the world" attitude that will ignite your masculine fires and help you to conquer and achieve anything you set your mind to.

Learning to embrace *no* will develop your mental toughness. And as long as you can give people the freedom to disagree, reject, dislike, and oppose you without taking it personally or allowing it to weaken your resolve, you will tap into a new source of power that few men ever realize in their lifetime.

I have a suggestion to make embracing *no* a part of your daily life. Whatever your desired goal is, try sharing your goal with those you can trust in order to hold yourself accountable. Naturally, you will feel a sense of fear of failure and fear of rejection based on just how crazy and outlandish YOU think your goal is, but do it anyway.

I don't know many guys who enjoy being told that he can't be, do, or have something that he ardently wants to be, do, or have. In fact, I don't know any guy who likes being told that something he really wants in life is beyond him and totally out of his reach. Real men don't like it, and neither should you. So try to use the word *no* as fuel to catapult you to greater success.

As long as the positive opinions you have of yourself and your goals are of higher quality than what other people think about you and your desires, you'll have no problem overcoming the world. It is actually at this point that your man transformation will reach a whole new plateau, and you'll have learned one of the most valuable skills that a man can possess.

You'll learn the power of *resilience*. And I can assure you, there's probably not a single woman out there who doesn't want to be with the kind of man who can stubbornly go after what he wants while maintaining an optimistic attitude in the process of doing so. Simply stated, embracing *no* will make you resilient. Becoming resilient will strengthen your character as a man. It makes you radiate masculine power and poise. A man with a strong character is highly attractive to a quality woman.

In a figurative sense, you'll be the kind of man that can take a punch to the face, fall on his backside, and have a big grin on his face as he immediately jumps back on his feet to deliver his knockout blow.

So learn to rely on faith while you navigate through life and take action consistently to get your needs and those of your loved ones met. You will face discouragement along the way and you will hear thousands of *no's*. But if you can maintain a positive attitude, stick to your guns, and keep moving forward, every *no* will help make a better man out of you.

And by learning to embrace *no*, almost overnight you'll become the kind of man that a woman can rely on and completely put her trust in.

CHAPTER 3:
How To Get Rid Of Your Insecurities

Take Responsibility by Becoming Your Own Man

Are you your own man or are you living the life that someone else designed for you? It's okay, take your time and really give it some thought.

When you were young you probably said what you wanted to say and did what you wanted to do regardless of what anyone else thought. When you were young you probably didn't care what people thought about your opinions about someone or something. You probably even wore anything you could get your hands on without worrying if someone was going to make fun of you.

You were fearless and perhaps somewhat reckless as well. You would climb high trees, jump high walls with a big drop at the other end with your friends, and even make fun of girls while having a blast just enjoying the thrill of being a boy.

But then one day all of that changed.

One day you became much more self-conscious about what others thought about you. You decided that it wasn't right to always state your opinions about something or someone. You decided that your choice of clothing might not be appropriate around your group of friends since they'd probably laugh at your natural selection. You decided that being adventurous outdoors and making fun of women for the sake of your own enjoyment might be dangerous to some degree, and you'd rather not face the negative outcome of either.

You became someone else's man, and in the process you lost your inner compass.

It's okay.

It's a natural process of male maturity. But the problem only remains when you fail to get your inner compass back.

Develop a Mind of Your Own

How sweet would it be if you were the kind of man that was completely free from the criticisms of others? How awesome would it be to be completely cool and confident in any situation simply because you had an inner locus of control? What if you weren't swayed to the left or to the right by popular opinion because you had an inner knowing that justified your course of action? What if you could act independently without having to doubt your decisions because people disagreed with you?

I think you know how powerful this kind of attitude is for a man to have.

Don't get me wrong, having an independent inner locus of control and direction does not mean that you're free from accountability or seeking the advice and wise counsel of others. All it means is that when you do seek advice and constructive criticism, you do so WILLINGLY by your own choice.

You submit to good advice because you choose to, and not because you feel obligated to in order to gain approval.

With an independent inner locus of control and direction, no man or woman can force you to do anything that you're not willing to do. So if you realize that it is necessary for you to seek out advice, you must <u>choose</u> to seek it. If it's necessary for you to get feedback on the decisions that you're making, you go out and get that feedback.

In other words, you're allowing others within your personal boundaries because YOU decide to. The mature man realizes when it's necessary to close his mind against all opposition and move forward with what he believes is right, and he also realizes when it's time to take a step back and open himself up to the RIGHT kind of influences to help him make BETTER decisions.

This is what it means to "be your own man."

Opening Up Your Mind

It's important for you to become a self-assured and self-reliant man that maintains his individuality in a world of thoughtless conformity. It's important especially in your relationship because a good woman is more willing to support a man that truly has a mind of his own.

She doesn't want to be with a man that falls prey to peer pressure. And she'd rather not spend her life with the kind of man that retreats into the shadows every time someone disagrees with his point of view.

Be a man, and stand your ground.

Stay focused on your path in life. As long as your

inner convictions are strong enough, that's all the motivation you'll need.

But let's not get out of hand. It's still important for you to know when to get some help, adjust your vision, and even change direction. Having personal boundaries means that you're in control of who or what you let into those boundaries in order to influence you in some way.

But how do you know when it's a good time to open up those boundaries to allow *positive* influence? Well, first of all, look at the results you're getting. If you've made a decision and decided to stick to it and you're not getting the kind of results that you want then it may be time for you to seek out wise counsel from someone who's already done what you want to do.

Another way to figure out if you need the opinions of others is by way of the quality of your relationships. Do you have any supporters? Do you have others, even a small few that are willing to help you to reach towards your desired goals and aspirations?

If no one is supporting you, and I mean NO ONE, then it may be time to sit back and re-evaluate the direction that you're headed and the decisions you've been making.

How to Kill Your Inner Weakling

Your number one enemy when trying to build a meaningful and powerful relationship with an amazing woman is going to be your <u>insecurities</u>. I know I'm making a bold statement here, but I truly believe that all relationship issues can be traced back to this one root cause.

All misunderstandings, communication problems, and lack of fulfillment whether you're with the woman you want or not stems from your own insecurities as a man and hers as a woman. If you're going to mature as a man, you're going to have to learn how to overcome these personal insecurities. You're going to have to become a master at killing your inner weakling.

Now, when I say *weakling* in this regard I'm referring to deep-rooted emotional issues that create guilt, doubt, anxiety, stress, timidity, frustration, and worry. I'm talking about all those little voices in your mind (yes, you do have them) that put you into a negative state of thinking whenever you ALLOW them to have their say.

If you don't get in control of your own thought processes, you are never going to have enough mental clarity to make good decisions. If your mind is being ruled by fear all of the time, then nothing you do will be good enough for anyone, not even yourself.

You'll feel self-defeated at every step of the way, soon becoming paralyzed and unable to make up your own mind about what you should do in life. This causes you to be open to outside influences, allowing anyone to have a say as to how you should handle things.

What's worse, since bad advice is usually the most readily available you'll only end up filling yourself up with even more negative input that tends to lead you down the wrong direction. My friend, it is this vicious cycle of thinking and acting that only enhances the power that your insecurities have over you.

And make no mistake…

If you don't feel secure within yourself, no woman will feel secure with you.

Even though I mention these insecurities as your inner weakling, it can still overpower your sense of logic since its power of influence lies in its ability to stir your *emotions*. Always keep this in mind, because whatever you allow into your mind can either make the weakling's influence over you stronger or weaker.

It's that simple.

Whatever you allow to influence you from the outside world will either enhance your own insecurities or it will reduce them to nothing. You have a CHOICE in the matter because YOU decide what goes into your mind.

So with this in mind, let's see what you can do to kill the inner weakling that is only making your life more difficult than it needs to be.

Create and Follow Your Code of Conduct

A man without a code of conduct to follow is like a castle without walls. Anyone or anything can intrude and destroy the sanctity of his mind and corrupt the clarity of his thoughts and the potency of his actions.

You need to have your own code of conduct. No matter what area of your life you're looking to improve on as a man, you NEED to have one.

This alone is more than enough to make a really great woman fall in love and stay in love with you simply because it shows her that you are unwilling to just sit back and accept anything from anybody. It shows her that you have goals and standards, and if she's the kind of woman that's worth your time and energy then she'll have her own goals and standards as well.

But more than that, your code of conduct acts like a set of rules or protocol by which you regulate your life. Although you may think that creating rules for yourself seems stifling, they actually help to liberate your thinking while bringing strength and vitality to your actions.

For example, if you don't know what's important to you in terms of financial success, you may be willing to settle for financial struggle and living from paycheck to pay check. On the other hand, if you don't have clear personal boundaries when it comes to <u>attaining</u> financial success, you may be willing to do underhanded or illegal things to achieve it.

Your code of conduct will help you to figure out what's important for you to be, do, and have in life, and also what things you're unwilling to compromise on.

For example, a personal rule of mine is that I'm willing to do whatever it takes to achieve the goals I've set for myself so long as it does not decrease the quality of life of someone else. I'm committed to being a successful man, but not at the expense of my health, meaningful relationships, my morals, and the well-being of others.

Another rule that I've adopted that has helped me immensely is: "I refuse to suffer." This means that whenever I find myself worrying, anxious, or frustrated about something, I remind myself that as a man I <u>choose</u> not to suffer in this way.

This quickly reminds me that the cure for worry and anxiety is *action*, and when I remember this I can always do something to bring about a change in the way I'm feeling. If there's really nothing I can do about the situation, I just relax my nerves, let it all go, and realize that it's out of my hands. I might as well relax if there's nothing I can do about it at that point, especially since "I refuse to suffer."

Having your own code of conduct will make you accountable to yourself first and then to others. To create your code, find a quiet spot where you will not be disturbed and begin to think about those things in life that are most important to you.

What are you unwilling to compromise on?

How will you treat others day in and day out?

In what manner will you conduct yourself around women?

How do you treat the woman in your life?

What do you want to bring about in your life?

What are you willing to die for?

What are you willing to die trying to accomplish?

Who are the people that are most important to you?

What are the morals, values, and ethics that you choose to live by?

How do you act under pressure?

How do you act around other men?

What kind of man are you?

Or better yet, what kind of man would you like to become?

Write everything down and fine-tune this list over time. Go over it as much as you can each day until it seeps deep into your subconscious mind. If you can get it in there, you win, since it will become a natural part of your behavior and you would have strengthened your inner compass.

Use your code as a self-affirmation that can replace those old broken records that play in your mind. You know the records I'm talking about... Those old broken records that remind you of how messed up you are, how you'll never be the kind of man you want to be, or even how you don't deserve her, etc. etc.

Yeah, those records...

We all have them in some form or fashion, and they suck big time. Your code of conduct will help to destroy this inner weakling because it will change the commitments you make to yourself and the conversations you have in your mind.

Trust me, it's important that you DO NOT skip this advice; make your code of conduct.

Without your own well-built code of conduct you will be a chameleon of a man. You'll be willing to change who you are just to fit in with others. You'll be an approval-seeking victim and you'll even be willing to accommodate others even if it means you have to suffer. You'll end up suffering from the nice-guy syndrome simply because your personal boundaries, or lack thereof, are not well defined.

Create your code and stick to it. Whenever external pressures begin to arise, go back to your code and remember why you made it. Don't doubt yourself if you believe that something is important to you. As men, we gain self-confidence and a boost in our self-esteem when we show integrity and act on what we believe is right.

One thing I should note, however, is that the time may come when you may want to change some things in your code of conduct, and that's fine. You're an evolving creature and you may come across some knowledge or wisdom that may challenge a belief that you have. It may actually be something that helps to expand your thinking and improve your life in some way.

So if you've given it some thought and something you've just learned seems more congruent with the man you'd like to be, put it into your code of conduct and make it a working part of your life.

Persistently following a code of conduct that evolves based on all that is good and right for your path will drastically improve your life in ways that you can't even imagine.

Study the Lives of Great Men You Admire

Honestly, I can think of no other way to rid yourself of past insecurities and motivate yourself to change into a more powerful and purposeful version of yourself than to study the lives of the great men that you admire. Whether it is in the form of biographies, autobiographies, documentaries, or even bits and pieces of media here and there, the lives of great men have much to teach us.

When you study the lives of men who have done great things in this world, you'll always notice that they were rarely ever universally popular in their stance on a particular issue or they rarely had everyone's support in what they were working towards. These were the men who against all odds remained true to themselves and true to their vision in order to accomplish greatly. They weren't easily swayed by the popular opinions of the day, but instead a strong inner compass that compelled them to press on against all adversity led them.

If you favor more recent examples of greatness then you may want to study the lives of those men who are still alive today but who are doing great things to move humanity forward.

If you'd like to build a great business, study the lives of great entrepreneurs and captains of industry. If you'd like to create a great work of art, consider inspiring yourself by studying the lives and works of other great artists. And even if all you want is to become a better man, study the lives of men who were great leaders in both their public duties and in their homes. Let their stories inspire and encourage you to make your vision grand, to set your bar high, and to think BIG when it comes to reaching your highest potentials.

I mention this as a great way to overcome your inner weakling because in the stories of great men you'll discover how they struggled with their own insecurities, self-doubt, and unwarranted fears from time to time. You'll discover how these men overcame such insecurities to accomplish greatly and how they acted courageously in spite of fear.

Trust me on this one, reading the right biography of a great man at the right time in your life when you need it most will probably teach you far more about manliness, leadership, and decision-making then most of those fluffy self-help books out there.

The stories of great leaders and achievers can provide you with wisdom and deep insights in overcoming your own inner weakling. Some of them might even put some hair on your chest and a bit of fire in your belly at the same time.

How to Destroy All Negative Influences

Make it a practice to close your mind against all negative influences that are internal and external to you. Stop listening to the wisdom of the crowds and adhere to your own inner locus of direction. Even more importantly, stop listening to that broken record in the back of your mind that keeps telling you things that fill you with the paralyzing feeling of fear.

It's important that I stress the point that fear is a powerful and overwhelming emotion when it takes hold in the mind. It can ruin your career, your business, your relationships, and your health. Fear is essentially the most debilitating force in this world. Every negative and sinister thing that exists in our society today is the result of fear.

Keep this in mind the next time those broken records play in the back of your mind, because you being fearful is not going to help ANYONE in this world.

Okay, I've stepped down from my little soapbox...

Now that I've gotten that off of my chest, let's see what we can do to reduce the amount of negative influences that we download from the outside world and upload into our own minds.

Fine-Tune Your Information Diet

I've got news for you. Everything you consume in the form of information is having an effect on your ability to function as a man.

Everything!

From the newspapers you read every day to the music that you choose to listen to. Whatever you put into your mind has to go someplace and do something. By repetition the information goes into your subconscious mind and becomes a working part of who you are and what you believe.

Make an effort to really sit down and analyze all of the inputs in your life. From the friends that you associate with to the magazines that you read, really think and ask yourself, "Is this person, place, or thing helping me to become the man that I really want to be? Is this thing a positive or negative influence in my life?"

Develop the habit of asking yourself this one question especially:

"Does this add value to my life?"

Be honest with yourself because we're constantly being bombarded with information every single day. You'd be surprised at what's being poured into your mind, and if you're not careful you'll find yourself being influenced in ways you never really wanted to. I'm not saying to shut out the entire world and become a hermit, but you do have the power to at least regulate some if not most of what you consume in the form of information.

Just how eating unhealthy food over a long period of time will be detrimental to your physical well-being, consuming negativity in the form of information over a long period of time will be detrimental to your emotional and psychological well-being.

Whatever you put into your mind, whether good or bad will take root. Think of the information you consume as mental seeds that grow into enormous trees and forests in your mind. You can choose to have a forest of productive and powerful thoughts or a forest of crap.

Always remember, garbage in, garbage out.

That's just the way it is.

Be Selective In Seeking Advice

Become extremely selective in whose advice you seek and how much of it you accept. Never take everything someone says as gospel. When you're getting some good advice from others, take what you need and abandon what doesn't work or what doesn't line up with your values, priorities, and code of conduct.

Always be willing to analyze and give thought to the advice of others. And yes, I'm including myself as well. Even though I'm pretty sure that the advice I'm presenting to you is pretty top-notch, you don't have to listen to EVERYTHING I have to say. Some things may not be important to you at this time in your life or maybe this advice is working for you already.

"If it ain't broke don't fix it", right?

Well, not really. But if you don't need it, don't use it.

Be open, but highly selective in your pursuit of knowledge and wisdom because it's always best that you hear and learn from the best. Learn from others and apply their lessons to your life based on your unique situation. If it works, keep it, if it doesn't, drop it.

Don't allow yourself to suffer because you think that you need to follow someone's advice to the letter. Get as much good advice as you can, but remember that you'll overcome your own insecurities and strengthen your inner compass more if you learn to rely on what feels right to you based on your own intuition and past experiences.

Cut the Social Consensus Umbilical Cord

Give up the need to have your likes, dislikes, decisions, and plans preapproved by everyone in your social group. Stop seeking the approval of others in the things you do and the decisions that you feel strongly about. Allow yourself the pleasure of having a mind of your own.

Today, we have things like Facebook and Twitter that allow us to share our ideas and opinions with one another and have them judged immediately by our own social groups. If we like a movie, we can see who else likes the movie. If we dislike a particular article we can see who else dislikes it.

We live in a societal box in many ways in which it can be difficult at times to know exactly what is true to us or if we're merely following the crowd. If you're always basing your decisions on the social consensus, you'll never be free to become the kind of man you really want to become simply because you're not in possession of your own mind.

Resist the desire to have others like the same things you do so that you can feel validated by the group. Needing to have so much feedback from society will only add to your insecurities because you'll always be wondering if you're doing things right.

Instead of drowning out your own inner voice, learn to listen to it by refusing to become an opinion gatherer. Follow your inner compass and become so comfortable in your own skin that it doesn't matter if those you associate with agree with you or not. Because in the end, you'll find that the only thing that really matters is your own inner convictions.

The Power of Masculine Sexual Confidence

Regardless of what you've heard, women think about sex...A LOT, and it is quite important to them. Seriously, pick up a women's magazine (if you dare) and check out just how many articles focus on sex alone.

No matter what stage you are in your relationship with a woman she has probably thought about it at some point and to some degree. Whether it's now or in the future, your ability to create and maintain sexual desire in her will be linked to your own masculine sexual confidence.

This may come as a shock to you...but the more in-touch and in control you are of your own inner animal, the more you will communicate sexual confidence to a woman. A woman will probably never tell you this...but she wants you to be able to stay in control of your animal AND be able to LOSE control of it when the timing is right and when your commitment is guaranteed.

The better you can communicate this paradox to a

woman, the more responsive she will be and the more she will desire everything that you have to offer her as a man. Your sexual confidence is important to a woman because it reveals to her whether or not you're capable of fulfilling her sexual needs, both physical and emotional. As you interact with any woman, she's subconsciously reading your every word and action to pick up whether or not you "get it" as a man.

What she's subconsciously trying to figure out is:

When the time comes, can this guy meet my deepest sexual needs?

This is where learning how to *feel* sexually confident is effective because it caters to the primal female brain. In fact, a lot of things we do as human beings can find root in the mating game, so to speak. The level of sexual responsiveness a woman gives to you may reveal just how much sexual confidence you're actually communicating.

That is, if you're communicating any at all.

Sexual Confidence and Attraction

Sexual confidence as a man is an important aspect of being a naturally attractive man simply because in order to create desire within a woman you are going to have to be comfortable with the idea of being able to fulfill her physical and emotional needs. It's impossible for you to exude *masculine chivalry* if you don't feel a sense of confidence in your ability to please a woman sexually. How can you be both her lover and her protector if you're unable to accept the fact that:

You are a MAN and you have needs, such as sex. She is a woman and she has needs, such as YOUR DESIRE.

Read those last two sentences again and see if it really clicks for you. Understanding and the accepting these facts are the first steps to boosting your sexual confidence. So begin to see yourself as being strong and capable of romancing the woman of your choice. Don't be ashamed of your sexual desires, it's natural.

Of course, that doesn't mean that you should let your primal instincts get the best of you. For what is a man if he lacks self-control? I believe that there's a right and wrong time for everything and the same applies for sex. The point of being sexually confident is not to try and "force" yourself on a woman, but it's more about how you *communicate* your sexual desires for her. You can be creepy about it, or you can be classy. It's all up to how you confident and in-control you are as a man.

CHAPTER 4:
On Becoming A Capable And Confident Leader

Becoming a Better Leader for You and Her

The kind of woman that will make your life much more fulfilling is the kind of woman that wants to be led by a man who knows how to deal with conflict and how to make intelligent decisions.

Sound judgment and poise are two traits that a good leader must possess. The better you become at creating win-win solutions when dealing with others and exercising emotional control, the more effective your decision making will be. Women are biologically designed to seek out a leader to give themselves to both physically and emotionally.

Think about it, because this also applies in the animal kingdom just as it does in the human world. In the animal kingdom, the alpha male gets to pick the best of the bunch. He decides what territory he wants and which females he wants to mate with. Nature has designed a system whereby the best males get to procreate and basically run the show. The alpha male is the one who takes control of a group, passes on his genes, and leads and protects the group that he's taken control of.

Truly, only the strong survive.

Although things aren't as primal in the human world, it's still pretty much based on the same premise. Men who are highly successful and highly respected in society have the ability to do things other men cannot do, to go places they cannot go, and to have the kinds of women that other men simply cannot have.

But where most guys go wrong is that they focus on the OUTWARD signs of male dominance and see that as the only means to attract and keep a high-quality woman in their life. They think that ridiculous good looks, fame, or fortune are their ticket to getting and keeping the woman of their dreams.

They've been told a lie.

The outward manifestations of success and power all represent something else. Any guy who is willing to take the journey, and begin working on becoming the best version of himself can harness this 'something else'.

Things such as wealth, power, fame, and physical attractiveness simply represent *leadership* in some form or another. It illustrates a guy who stands out from the crowd, someone to admire, to respect, and to follow.

But luckily, those of us who may not be ridiculously good-looking, wealthy, or well-known still have a fighting chance at attracting and keeping a woman that is gorgeous, intelligent, loyal, and loving. Through developing leadership qualities you will find that not only will a woman become naturally drawn to you, but that you'll also begin to attract more SUCCESS into your life.

How to Remain Calm in Conflict

Learning how to effectively handle conflict is essential if a good woman is ever going to place her confidence in you as a capable leader. Just like building muscles, you'll build emotional strength and resilience the more you exercise your decision-making ability in and out of conflict. And just like the more weights you use, the more muscle you can build; the more intense the conflict, the more emotional poise you can develop.

The next time you're faced with a difficult situation, learn to stand outside of it and "pause". Instead of reacting to your environment, choose a response. This is where your powerful subconscious mind comes into play. Create a powerful affirmation or some other form of positive self-talk that will make you aware of how you act and respond in a difficult situation.

Your phrase MUST be present tense and fill you with emotion when you say or think of it. For example, something like:

"I am cool, calm, confident, and in control. Nothing or no one can cause me to lose my composure. I am a self-assured leader, and I make the best decisions at all times. When everyone around me is losing control, I am becoming cooler and calmer. I am the go-to guy when things get out of hand. I'm THE MAN, and everybody knows it."

This is a working basis for a powerful affirmation or self-talk of your own, but just remember that it should fill you with emotion the more you repeat it to yourself. I can guarantee you that if you develop the habit of repeating a set of positive self-talks to yourself in private and even when a conflict arises, you WILL begin to see positive results.

I want to suggest a book that I'd advise you to read at least twice. It's called, *What To Say When You Talk*

To Yourself, and it was written by best-selling author, Dr. Shad Helmstetter. The title of the book basically says it all really, but he goes into lots of detail on how to transform your life by changing the conversations you have with yourself.

Yes, by changing the conversations you have with yourself. Basically, your self-talk literally regulates your thinking which in turn regulates your actions, which in turn gives you the results in your life. In other words, when you change your self-talk, you'll change your life.

It's a rollicking read.

But enough about Shad, and let's get back to you...

If the set of phrases I suggested earlier seem a bit too long to say to yourself when you get into some sort of conflict or stressful situation, just use a shorter version:

"I am in control of my emotions. I am self-confident and self-assured, and I make excellent decisions. I am a fearless man with immense poise and power."

Make it a practice to use self-talk in both private and public settings. When you're alone, repeat it to yourself as a mantra. Get emotional about it and picture yourself as an immovable mountain surrounded by a thunderous storm. Seriously, visualizing helps a lot to convey the message of power and poise to your subconscious.

Experiment with it and see what works for you. But don't overlook it as some psychobabble fix that won't get you results. Trust me, the mind is more powerful than most of us realize. Since your desire is to become the perfect guy to the woman of your dreams, you'll need to use its incredible power to the utmost to get the results you really want.

Learning to Make Better Decisions

The man who takes charge and shows initiative in doing things is an alluring catch to a high-quality woman. But how do you become the kind of man who makes good decisions consistently? Well, there are two ways that I personally know about and that have worked for me. Here they are:

First, study the lives of other leaders and great men that live or have lived prosperous and successful lives so you can learn what choices they made throughout their life. Read books written with the intention of improving your leadership skills as well, as becoming a leader requires masterful decision making skills.

Secondly, learn to make more decisions, a whole lot more. Take the initiative when the opportunity arises by making a conscious effort to offer up and execute a solution to a problem.

As I've mentioned earlier, the biographies of great men as well as the books written by them are filled with insight and wisdom for those of us wanting to become better decision-makers. Reading about such individuals will help to furnish your mind with lots of examples of what choices these men made when faced with adversity and insurmountable circumstances.

Not only will the reading of books on and by great men help you to make better decisions, but you'll be developing a habit that will make you far more successful in life and far more attractive to a high-quality woman. Your thinking will be so unique and different from most of the guys around you that she won't be able to resist taking an interest in you.

The other option to use with the first is to make more tough decisions, and make them while being conscious of the fact that you are at that very moment making a tough decision. Use the direct approach and refuse to pussyfoot around an issue.

When you become aware of the amount of decisions that you make on a day-to-day basis, you put yourself in a state of creative power. What this means is that you'll begin to realize that you are responsible for your results in life. You are responsible for your future. You are the master of your fate, the captain of your soul.

As you make more of these decisions day to day, make them unflinchingly. If you decide upon a course of action and it doesn't work out, don't worry yourself about it. Just remind yourself that you'll make a much better decision the next time around (this is where using powerful positive self-talk will come in handy).

Remember, make the tough call and make it consciously. Some decisions you'll have to make will not help you to win a popularity contest. But the goal is not to be liked, the goal is to have integrity with yourself and direct your own course.

Be a man.

A high-quality woman loves a man who can be counted on to make the tough decisions when required. Why? Well, for one, it shows her that you're confident, self-directed, and able to commit to things. And secondly, she wants a man in her life to make those tough decisions that she probably wouldn't want to make.

Be that man.

Because, when a man knows what direction he's headed in, he becomes much more attractive to the opposite sex. When he knows where he's going in life he's able to make better decisions on a daily basis.

This doesn't mean that his decisions become easier to make, but it does mean that he has much more clarity to make better decisions. This is important because if you want to become the kind of man that a woman can follow confidently then you're going to have to become extremely comfortable making a lot of tough decisions that are important to your life's purpose.

Why Every Man Needs to Know His Purpose and Path in Life

Okay, so now we've come to what I think may be the single most important aspect of a man's life…

…His purpose.

If you have no purpose, no path, and no mission in life, then it will be impossible for you to ever reach your highest potentials and become the kind of man that a quality woman can fully give of herself to. The purposeless man is merely a leaf that blows with the wind. He has no branch and no root in which to nourish and strengthen himself. He simply moves from place to place never knowing true happiness and fulfillment in life.

The man without a purpose is neither master of his fate nor the captain of his soul. He is merely a minion, a pawn, and a tool for men who know what they want out of life and who are determined to get it.

If you follow no other advice about becoming a better man, at least follow this one:

Find your path in life and be determined to stay on that path no matter what.

Hopefully you'll still read the rest of this book after I say this but...

Finding your path in life and staying on that path is more than enough to transform you into the kind of man that a woman will respect, admire, desire, and treat like a king. Not only that, if you haven't already found the right woman, finding your path will make you irresistible to the kind of woman who is essentially perfect for your particular life's journey.

So with this in mind, there are two extremely important questions that every man MUST ask himself:

1. Where am I going? And...

2. Who will go with me?

A man should never ask these questions in the wrong order because the success and happiness you find in your life's mission will have an effect on your relationship with the woman you choose to be with. If you're unhappy and unfulfilled because you've taken a path that is not your own, chances are you'll be unhappy and unfulfilled in your relationship and more than likely, your woman of choice may also feel unhappy and unfulfilled with you.

Purpose and a Labor of Love

Although your purpose or your mission in life is not the same thing as a job or career, they are inexorably linked to one another.

The truth of the matter is, you can probably engage in various kinds of work that can bring you fulfillment, happiness, and great success, and you may even find yourself in different careers at different points in your life. If you've still been able to find enjoyment and success in your job and career choices then perhaps you're living with purpose but you just didn't realize it.

Also, take into consideration that different kinds of work may bring you different levels of satisfaction depending on your own strengths and interests and the nature of the work.

For example, if you're a highly sociable person who'd rather form relationships and help others to form relationships than fix things, you'll find that you're happiest at your computer technician support job when you're interacting with users and customers as opposed to when you actually have to fix their PC's.

Now, let's say that you find yourself in a job or career that required less fixing of technical things but more fixing of human relationships, you'll probably have far more satisfaction in your work and far more passion for what it is you do.

If you were a marriage counselor or even a deal-maker in a big corporation you'd probably become the top dog in your field rather quickly simply because on a day to day basis you'd be involved in work that easily brought out your natural strengths and talents.

The idea is to find a labor of love that uses your strengths and talents at least eighty percent to one-hundred percent of the time. Obviously, the more your work uses your natural strengths and abilities the more satisfaction and enjoyment you will gain from it.

And make no mistake; every man needs a labor of love. I repeat; he NEEDS a labor of love in order to be fully satisfied with his lot in life. This is why it's so important for him to at least have a plan for his life or be consumed in a labor of love before he attempts to attract the right woman for himself. He'll already be on his chosen path, and if she is the right woman for him, she will fall in love with that path as well.

When a man is engaged in a life work that is not suitable to his natural interests and talents he remains a restless creature. And sadly, though he may have the most wonderful woman at his side, if he cannot find his own path, one that fills him with deep meaning and happiness, she can never make him truly happy and complete.

It's important for you as a man to find that which

you love to do and that which you can do. But don't be confused; the thing you may do exceptionally well may not be the thing that you can do stupendously well. Find that thing that will take you from good to great and commit to it.

Love What You Do...and Do What You Love

Sometimes fate deals us a rough hand in that we spend most of our lives engaged in work that doesn't satisfy us as much as we'd like. Day in and day out we may feel frustrated, depressed, and a sense of hopelessness thinking that "this is it", as we wonder if this is all that life has to offer.

I'm speaking from personal experience here, as I've been in this sort of predicament for a very long period of time in my own life. Amazingly, I was only able to find and keep the woman of my dreams after I started on the path that was more in tune with what I wanted out of life. To this day, she loves the man I am partly because I've committed myself to maximizing my potential and living a purposeful life.

Living with purpose by finding creative ways to add value to the world by doing what you love to do will bring you an uncommon success that few men ever realize. By committing yourself to bringing out your best in work that is congenial to your particular genius, your life will begin to change dramatically.

Why is this so? Well, by doing what you love you'll be giving off something that no human being is immune to. And that thing is...*enthusiasm*.

Your enthusiasm breeds more enthusiasm until you'll find yourself surrounded by relationships with other people who will only want to add value to your life. The more enthusiasm you have for your work, the more likely you are to share this enthusiasm with your woman.

Let's put it this way; she loves it when you're in love with something (your mission in life) OTHER than just her. A good woman who's right for you will appreciate you much more when you're following your dreams passionately. In fact, the minute you lose focus on your life's mission she's going to try to whip you back into shape. But if she cannot get through to you, she'll slowly but surely begin to lose her respect and admiration for you.

She probably won't tell you this (if she even knows), but it's important to her that you have something in your life that you've committed yourself to first and foremost, <u>even before you commit to her</u>. Your calling, your mission, or your path in life will draw her in and KEEP her at your side on your life's journey.

So if you're not currently engaged in work that you care about, it's imperative to your relationship success that you find out what it is that you really want to do in terms of your life's mission and life's work. Because as I've said before, this may be the most important thing you can do to become a better man that a good woman will truly respect and deeply admire.

The Secret to Being an Irresistible Catch

The secret to gaining and maintaining the love, admiration, respect, and desire of a quality woman is to continuously <u>evolve</u> into a better man. As a high-quality man you should never stop growing. You should never stop evolving consciously. As a man, you should always be seeking the next level, a better paradigm, and a higher ideal as you live your life.

In short, this is the path of leadership.

In fact, I could probably sum up this entire book with this one idea:

Women are attracted to men who illustrate the traits and qualities of leadership. A good woman will choose to follow and trust a man who is consciously following the path of leadership. Her love, respect, and desire for him will continue to grow so long as he can captivate her mind, body, and soul by making her an irreplaceable partner in his own grand adventure.

A good woman wants a man who can lead her, one who can make decisions. She wants a man she can place her confidence in, and she wants him to take her for who she is, and to love her deeply and romantically. To keep her captivated, you must choose to evolve.

This kind of commitment for on-going development will captivate and fascinate her continuously. Your desire to improve yourself alone is a turn-on for her simply because women are designed to be our indispensible counterparts. They are designed to want to assist us in becoming the best version of ourselves. And by committing yourself to such a path, you automatically become irresistible to her.

But even without getting women involved, the desire to become a better man is a noble goal. It requires a dedication to continuous high-character development that is specific for a man.

But what does it takes to develop a mature masculine character that will captivate a great woman for life? What does it take to have that masculine feeling of power that can only come from taking responsibility for their lives and pursuing their own path?

Let's dive in and find out, shall we?

Take Responsibility for Your Life

People don't give you responsibilities when you're a man. Even if they're "forced" upon you, you won't be able to perform at your highest until you "take" it upon yourself. Leaders TAKE responsibilities, they don't wait for it to be given to them.

I know we've gone through this before in the first section of the book, but this must be repeated. Taking responsibility is the first and most important factor in a man's development if he wants to rid himself of the whiny little boy inside of him. A man must learn to avoid blaming people and circumstances for his results and should instead take full responsibility for his entire life.

Learn to take ownership of the decisions you've

made. Accept the fact that you are where you are in life because of the decisions that you've made, and that the outcome of your tomorrow will be based on the decisions you make today. Always take ownership of the truth that your life is whatever YOU make of it, past present, and future.

A priceless woman of quality will find it increasingly difficult to deal with a man who always complains, whines, and criticizes everyone and the world around him. If your personality attracted her, but you still retain the boyish attitude of blame and playing the victim, she'll soon find herself losing her desire for you.

This is a slow and painful death.

To take responsibility in your life, first accept everything the way it is. No matter what your life looks like, just accept it as the outcome of your decisions and begin planning ways to improve it. This will bring you much peace of mind and a better sense of control over the future outcomes in your life.

Do Not Complain...Ever!

What's the fastest way to lose a woman's respect? Simple, just whine, moan, and complain about everything and everyone all the time. She'll be out of there faster than a speeding bullet. Nothing is more unattractive to a woman (or appalling to other men) than a man who's always complaining and criticizing the world around him. Such men make themselves out to be victims in the world, as if they have absolutely no control over their lives and their fate.

If you suffer from this disease of the mind, then I'll bet you probably always have a feeling of powerlessness that you just can't seem to shake. If you want to develop more leadership traits and keep your woman captivated, then stop complaining. Become aware of it, and refuse to engage in it. Learn to step outside of yourself for a minute and watch yourself falling prey to the victim's mindset.

As soon as you see it for what it is, powerlessness, stop it.

Sometimes we complain aloud and sometimes we do so in our own minds. The process of eradicating this disease begins by keeping your complaints to yourself, and soon after awhile you will learn to resist the complaining mindset entirely. Instead of succumbing to this victim mindset, learn to maintain a positive mental attitude by cultivating the habit of living a life of <u>deep gratitude</u>.

The best way to go about this is to count your blessings daily and find things to be grateful for. If you begin to use the first few minutes of every morning to think of all the things you're grateful for you'll begin to find much more enjoyment and opportunities in the world around you.

You'll actually end up developing a positive mental attitude. This is an attitude that can handle life's challenges with enthusiasm, and it is HIGHLY attractive to women.

Find Your Path...and Never Stray From It

Ask several men you know what their path in life is and most of them probably can't give you a clear and concise answer. A man without a clear path in life is simply wandering through the world aimlessly and without any direction. No good woman in her right mind is going to want to come along for that ride, at least not for long.

Knowing your purpose and following your own unique path in life will give you a deep sense of what it means to be committed to something bigger than yourself. It will give you a sense of duty and belonging that will motivate you to make positive changes in the world around you.

It will become your obsession, your mission in life to fulfill this purpose. You will lead a much happier and successful life once you've discovered your purpose and decide to stick to your path, no matter what. Having this unique path will make you much more effective in the world and much more attractive to the right woman who can help you in the achievement of your life's goals.

In fact, as long as you make your mission the most important aspect of your life, you'll never have to worry about losing the desire of the right woman simply because she will become highly interested and invested in you achieving what you set your heart on. And once you know what your purpose in life is, you'll find that it is easier to have peace of mind when things don't always go as you've planned.

Of course, discovering your own path may require some work on your part. It will take some effort in self-reflection and some soul searching. But trust me; it is definitely worth it in the long-run.

Quit Consuming and Become a Producer

No, this has nothing to do with movies, music, or becoming the next P. Diddy. This is about becoming a highly productive creator, builder, and provider in your family, community, and your slice of the world.

One of the key things that separate the mature male leader from the average Joe is that one is a producer and the other is a consumer. The average Joe takes in more than he gives out to the world in terms of value, but leaders give more than they receive in terms of value. The producer will always be greater than the consumer.

Think about it.

Nothing is more apparent in the lives of great men than the fact that they were men who learned how to create and provide massive amounts of value in their communities. They used their creative resources to build, pioneer, construct, and create new and valuable things. In other words, they were prolific producers.

If you want to grow and reach your highest potentials for yourself, your woman, and your community, you must become a prolific producer. The path to male leadership demands that a man cast off his childish ways of thinking in order to develop an attitude of prolific creativity.

Through the effective management of your time, money, and resources you can enhance your own levels of productivity and add more value to the world than what you take from it.

Master Your Fears

If there is one thing that will stop you from being successful in not just your relationships, but in any area of your life, it would be the fear of failure and the fear of criticism. A leader learns to overcome these fears by mastering his emotions. He knows that failure is just a step on the path to attainment, and that criticism is merely a sign that he is alive and doing something productive and worthwhile with his life.

If you cannot fail forward, you cannot succeed in any area. And if you don't learn how to handle criticism, then you won't be able to do anything that matters to anyone. In order to master your fears you must master your emotions. You can do this by changing your idea about failure itself.

Think about it.

Failure is rarely permanent.

Instead, see it as a stepping stone and a lesson learned. See it as something you MUST go through in order to achieve success. When it comes to criticism, if it's constructive, simply see it as a way to either improve on what you're doing. If not, pay it no mind. Negative criticism can only hurt you if you're too attached to what you're doing.

Instead, learn to love the process of becoming as opposed to the outcome. If you can do this you won't have to worry yourself about criticism again.

A leader doesn't need the approval of others, including women. However, if he's in a healthy relationship with the right woman, he will seek her counsel when the time calls for it. But otherwise he is self-approved first and foremost, and this shows in the clarity of his thinking and the powerful outcomes of his decisions.

Mastering your fears will become easier as you become a better man. As you grow into full knowledge of who you are and what you're capable of, you'll have a greater peace of mind when dealing with the many unknowns in your life.

Cultivate Masculine Courage

I can give you no better advice for attaining success in your relationship with your woman and in other areas of your life than this:

Challenge yourself consciously and consistently every single day of your life. This will build the most important characteristic found in ALL great leaders and highly successful individuals of society. It will build your courage.

We've probably covered this a dozen times already, but it cannot be said enough. A man's courage to do what is right, to follow his path in life, to stand up for what he believes in, and to be the best version of himself is his MOST attractive and desirable quality to a woman.

Courage can only be cultivated by consciously doing it. Courage is something you DO. It's not something you think about, it's an action you TAKE. A man can build units of his own courage by doing the things he's normally averse to doing.

I believe that self-confidence is merely the way we communicate our levels of courage to others. It's impossible to have one without the other. Though physical and intellectual courage are quite important, it is moral courage that is especially important to a woman.

Moral courage will give you the strength and ability to exercise all of your other virtues. It will help you to make the right decision regardless of what others may think of you. This is one of the most essential aspects that separate the average man from the man who leads others. The man with great amounts of courage is not afraid to say what must be said and to do what must be done. And any woman would be more than willing to place her confidence and trust in such a man.

Accept Yourself Now

It's amazing how I'm about to wrap everything up with this last piece of advice seeing as though your mission is to become a better man for the woman who's right for you. It may seem contradictory, but trust me, it isn't.

You MUST learn how to accept yourself for who you are and for where you are in life beginning today.

Even though your mission as a mature man is to constantly evolve and reach your highest potential, if you fail to accept yourself and find contentment in your present stage of development you won't be effective in becoming the best version of yourself.

All transformation begins with self-acceptance. You must learn to recognize your present value in the present state you're in, because if you don't you'll continually thwart yourself whenever you fall short of your development goals and personal vision.

Forgive yourself magnanimously every single day. Give yourself a break for Pete's sake and refuse to berate yourself for any reason whatsoever. Stop worrying about what other guys are doing and stay focused on what is right for you at your stage of growth and development.

Become a master at self-acceptance by being grateful for what you have. Master the art of showing gratitude in your daily life and your life will change drastically.

Here's a life-changing tip; if you don't take anything else from this book (which I doubt), and this is the only thing that you learn, you WILL enjoy better relationships in every area of your life:

Cultivate the habit of being grateful for your life just as it is today, and how you'd like it to be in the future. Make it a HABIT to see the positive side of things, and develop an optimistic disposition towards life. Show your gratitude in how you live your life and EXPECT good things to happen to you.

And yes, it is quite possible to grow into a more capable and confident man while being content with who you are right now. Simply focus on your strengths and the things you like about yourself. All it takes is a determination to always strive for the best, balanced with the determination to always forgive yourself quickly whenever you do fall short. And trust me, you WILL fall short from time to time, but that's all right.

A good woman doesn't want a perfect man per se; she just wants a man who's perfect for her. The mere fact that you've dedicated yourself to her and to a path of continuous personal growth is all that she needs to admire, respect, and stay in love with you for as long as you desire.

Continuously Seek Wisdom

I'd just like to end our talk with one final piece of advice:

Don't be afraid to get good advice that can help you to improve yourself and your relationship.

Now, if you've read this book then you obviously don't have that problem, but this is just a reminder. Too often we decide to follow a certain path thinking that we've got it all figured out or that we'll just "go with the flow."

Although going with the flow can be fun, there's nothing more reassuring than having knowledge by your side as your own personal guide. It's better to be prepared in any situation, no matter how much you think you may know already.

I know for me at least, good things only began to change in my love life when I began to seek out really good advice and apply it. Some of it was free, some of it I paid for, but in the end it was all worth it.

As men we can be a bit hard-headed and prideful, especially when it comes to getting this area of our lives handled. But nonetheless, when a man decides to arm himself with a bit (or a lot) of knowledge, a whole new world of possibilities begins to open up for him.

When it comes to his relationship with his ideal woman, the more he educates himself, the more valuable he becomes to her.

So remember to keep on learning and to continue on your own personal development path towards maturing as a man. It'll make your romantic life much richer and more fulfilling in the long-run. Do this and the right woman will see you as an irresistible catch; the kind of man that she'd rather not live her life without.

About Bruce Bryans

Bruce is a successful writer, website publisher, and author. He has written many articles for various online publications and enjoys sharing the triumphs (and failures) of his love life with anyone who enjoys a good laugh or a life lesson.

When he isn't tucked away in some corner of his house writing a literary masterpiece (or so he thinks!), Bruce spends most of his time engaged in his hobbies or being a romantic nuisance to the love of his life. And after spending most of his twenties studying books about psychology, seduction, dating, and relationships, he's happy to finally have a gorgeous, exotic, sun-kissed goddess with a heart of gold to share his life with.

If you have any questions, comments, or you'd just like to say a quick "thanks", you can reach him at: brucebryansbooks@gmail.com

Best Books by Bruce Bryans:

Below is a short list of some of my other books that you can find on Amazon.com. Here's the link to my book list where you can access all of the books listed:

http://www.amazon.com/author/brucebryans

101 Things Your Dad Never Told You About Men: The Good, Bad, And Ugly Things Men Want And Think About Women And Relationships

In *101 Things Your Dad Never Told You About Men*, you'll learn what high-quality men want from women and what they think about love, sex, and romance. You'll learn how to seduce the man you want or captivate the man you love because you'll know exactly what makes him tick.

Attract The Right Girl: How To Find Your Perfect Girl And Make Her Chase You For A Relationship

In *Attract The Right Girl*, you'll discover how to find and choose an amazing girlfriend (who's perfect for you) and how to spark the kind of attraction that'll lead to a long-term relationship with her.

Find Your Path: A Short Guide To Living With Purpose And Being Your Own Man...No Matter What People Think

In *Find Your Path*, you'll discover how to find your mission in life and how to become a much more self-assured man of purpose and inner conviction.

How To Be A Better Boyfriend: Win Your Dream Girl's Heart, Master Her Emotions, And Keep Her Helplessly Attracted (And Loyal) To You

In *How To Be A Better Boyfriend*, you'll discover how to cultivate a rock-solid, mind-blowing, romantic relationship with your dream girl, and what to do to avoid all the drama, bad girlfriend (or wife) behavior, and game playing that many "nice guys" often fall prey to in relationships.

How To Get Your Wife In The Mood: Quick And Easy Tips For Seducing Your Wife And Making Her BEG You For Sex

In *How To Get Your Wife In The Mood*, you'll discover the relationship secrets used by some of the most blissful couples in the world as well as romantic hacks that'll help you to get all the sex you want from your wife and make it seem like it was all HER idea.

Meet Her To Keep Her: The 10 Biggest Mistakes That Prevent Most Guys From Attracting And KEEPING An Amazing Girlfriend

In *Meet Her To Keep Her*, you'll learn the ten dating mistakes that stop most guys from attracting and keeping a 'Total 10 girlfriend' and how to overcome them.

What Women Want In A Man: How To Become The Confident Man That Women Respect, Desire Sexually, And Want To OBEY…In Every Way

In *What Women Want In A Man*, you'll learn how to become a high-quality, self-confident man that can naturally attract a good woman, maintain her sexual attraction to you, and keep her "well-trained" in a relationship.

Find Your Path: A Short Guide To Living With Purpose And Being Your Own Man...No Matter What People Think

In *Find Your Path*, you'll discover how to find your mission in life and how to become a much more self-assured man of purpose and inner conviction.

Make Him BEG For Your Attention: 75 Communication Secrets For Captivating Men And Getting The Love And Commitment You Deserve

In *Make Him BEG For Your Attention*, you'll discover how to talk to a man so that he listens to you, opens up to you, and gives you what you want without a fuss.

Thank You

Before you go, I'd like to say "thank you" for purchasing my book.

I know you could have picked from dozens of books on understanding women, but you took a chance on my guide and for that I'm extremely grateful. So thanks again for purchasing this book and reading all the way to the end.

Now, IF you liked this book I'm going to need your help!

Please take a moment to leave a review for this book on Amazon. Your feedback will help me to continue to write the kind of books that helps you get results. And if you so happen to love this book, then please let me know!

25475813R00063

Made in the USA
Lexington, KY
25 August 2013